Anemone

Anemone

THE WINDFLOWER

J.Limbu

ISBN- 13: 978-9937-0-2022-0
Visit the author's website at www.strangerstale.com

All illustrations by J. Limbu
Edited by Steve Coonrod
Publisher: Ocean Gurung

ACKNOWLEDGMENT

It is and it will be my greatest pleasure to convey my gratitude to those people whose name may not all be enumerated here but have encouraged me and made 'Anemone' possible to exist. I'm very much grateful for their assistance and contributions; it could have not been achievable without it. They therefore, are humbly appreciated and acknowledged within the grasp of my heart. However, I would like to express my deepest regard and indebtedness particularly to the following:

Mr. Anil Nembang, Mr. Steve Coonrod, Mrs. Josephine Boyce, Mrs. Shabu Limbu and Mrs. Ocean Gurung for their endless support, kind and understanding spirit during the course of making.

To my family, relatives, friends, and others who in one way or another shared their support, either morally, financially and physically, thank you.

J.Limbu

<u>CONTENTS</u>

Chapter   He

INTRODUCTION

To write as to give a place or the theatre- his body, for those inextricable clamours wailing inside of him, which demanded his attention for his whole life or perhaps somehow to contain his own demons that slept beside his dreams but no longer, writing could've kept his sanity balanced with the evoking insanity that fated to meet with him someday. He needed more than a simple language that was taught before him; he soon needed something more riveting to control his cascading emotion. He needed poetry- the powerful play, the beautiful notation as in the romance with words, the distinctive rhythm to value the delicate arts of our intense living, and so he began to rhyme…the verse- the prose of his living. He the poet…rose from himself.

"Less he was known for who he said to be, the poems of impenetrable obscurity was where he oath to be."
J. Limbu as self-titled (pain) is often known by reclusive behaviour or eccentric nature in his vicinity. And before as you and as many might frame him in some introvert anatomy; he has described himself as 'more of the nature than people'. So as personal or private he loves to keep himself, the poet has kept his rhymes with himself until now… but after what he has decided, the book you're holding is supposed to be the collection of the very poems he wrote and now it's yours to read. But why decide to reveal now? Because once he said, "Right now nothing could be more precious than these poems I've written; they are what I am". And as dearly he kept, he

doesn't want it to perish in the dust of age or get lost in old folders of machines.

The book Anemone (The Wind Flower) is not just the collection of poems which holds the meaning individually but what it means altogether. The author choosing this name is what makes this book more relatable to his enigmatic life. The title has its own definition being the windflower-Anemone. To understand more acutely; you'd have to learn the history from where the name came from and why he chose, what it means but besides his reticent; he reveals less, "It's about a great loss, the book- tragedy of mine and nothing suits better than the name Anemone."

CHAPTER

❧ She ❧

She: "How long is forever, my love?"
He: "Not so long… if I love you every day!"

FAREWELL

I hope you wake up smiling to the warm sun rays that peep through your window and tells you it's late. And while you hurry yourself to get down out of your bed and prepare yourself for another casual day with your friends and the world- your heart gets heavy and you realize something's missing; you would finally know there isn't me in your life anymore. Either way you would disperse those thoughts away like every time, like a bad memory, and smile again!

FEED ME LOVE

As she tucked her burning head into the cold stone river
Mistaking her heat as she blames underground
As the water felt bruised of her skin,
It swallowed her in depth from being deprived mean
As they both now share the story of coldness
Her submission brought love to the sea
She now saw the devil in the sky
As her eyes painted with good being
Where she just rose with tranquility,
She was in a ring of deceit
As it laid its lust to the beauty
She now thought angels are just a foul myth to keep.

PREVENTING MELANCHOLY SEASON

Take those pictures down now
Use that ember dance to erase the vow
Move them far but safe, move where it belongs
Getting caught bleeding her, you can't remunerate another
consequences on
It's not easy again to take my pace with untied lace-
While being confined from the things you're running from
So turn around from those frames and forget,
the feelings of those walls
You will be doomed if the same wind blows and the
atmosphere plays;
Cause no love is ordinary and certainly she wasn't.

COME AGAIN

The tree grew lonely when the birds flew
Twenty foot tall pride, damned its root
Friend or foe with times, they were-
Stationary birth could be cursed too
Why such fate among strangers, who meet-
We make oath for such betide, eternity they breach
Then they leave as per their heights, playful sky
What happens to the branch which went undraped?
Some feathers for farewell, or souvenir
In the wind or the storm-
Their songs will repeat every year.

SOMEONE YOU CAN'T LOVE

She does it like the rebel and she falls like the rain
Sadness flows within her, like the rivers through mountains
Poetry escapes between her lungs and she howls like the dead
She brings silence, like the atmosphere surrounding the vale
But she has no name or place
She's sadness, like one that foments through every human vein.

DARKEST OATH

She: "How can you feed me illusions in my best
consciousness.."

Reality: "I will give you the taste of love!"

SWEETHEART

"You have found yourself lonely again but the crowds of your friends do not take you home and still they do not know, nor your people whom you share your living. Perhaps, it's too heavy and too strong to even to share the whisper, the feelings that you hold within your frail dainty heart which eats your happiness slowly, little by little like a parasite that once you adored- when he promised you more. But the parasite now has become more than a disease that has done you more than just damage….it made a whole; a void, an emptiness.

When you stare at the empty walls of your home or amble upon the meaningless street where you mostly went awry, only to be filled with exasperating views that no longer serves you any purpose for living, and you think, certainly you can't keep up with this desperate reality that unfaired you and broke you like a porcelain bowl by the mere breeze of yesterday; how you missed his fingers playing on your hips.

It suffocates you; it decays your lungs now to think
you have to breathe only for yourself and none."

THE PINING TREE

Be with your love, be with her
Run, run, and do not look down oh
Careless feet, promise her a reach
Have you seen yourself, have you?
You grew old with the old town
You can only be young with she

So find her a shelter of spring
Lay her down in a bed of autumn sheets
Gaze in her eyes of smoky brume
And disappear from the earthly duty

Underneath her dress, beneath her body
There lies a sea, where you're always free
Swim away, drift to a new valley
I know there lays a place
Beyond dreams and fantasy
Let's meet in our virtue and may our apathy rest.

COLORS OF TEARS

Where shall I find you If I no longer be needed in your heart
Where shall I be after the abandonment reaches my seek?
But if no women's heart resides, my love essence is but
treachery
This is all of me in these parts of tragedy

It's the part of getting used to, the weight of memory
And if you stand alone with your dreams, I am weak
But if what you adore must admire you for living
Have you all now betrayed me?

Life itself is all in these unfamiliar strings- attached
Waiting to be chained and some to be removed
If someone like me strives after detachment
Someone will find everything new

But my life should also proceed if for you it has already
Come; let's invite the eminent sadness or reverse
I, once your lover, don't exist and you my everything, don't live
Then the place we met didn't hold and the moments are now
perished!

ANCHORAGE

The wind died and the butterflies flew
Petals that fell with the gust of the breeze-
She stood wondering with the hues…

The beautiful blue skies, they've turned grey
She closed her eyes and the rain came
They rejoiced all by savoring her
While she exchanged her symphony into two

Both drowned in inescapable flame,
That burnt her within, inside her haze
"Come closer" she said, "come to feel"
Who dwells within me for hours, what's her tale.

SAVE ME FROM THE THINGS THAT I LOVE, LOVED

If all the flowers, I painted to you
Have now turned grey
Let me take the blame for their decay
Cause the one I wanted to give, permanent
You've gone too far to receive; I am late
But do not doubt my virtue from then, it was all I gave
But for the hindrance to my wounded love,
Do all the lovers pay for their need and crave

YOU ARE MISSED BY ME

Somebody save me from the nightmare
Someone stole my lullaby
Forgive me, if I am trying to find
The place where old butterflies die

If she must choose to dream away-
Missing you would be a farewell
Where if existence should disappear in moments
Then
I shall sleep, to be with you again!

THE WILDFLOWERS

Everyone remembered the flowers
But I wanted to see the leaves
I wanted to know how they feel
To be apart, to woe!

Swing me by your side
Mocking petals of daughter's tree
Do you smoke colors?
Lusty bones, hallucinate me

In a lonely house, youths die
Only few children survived
But little Sarcodes died from the snow
None but the women who cared know

The delusional fumes choked
By the river bed in gold
As silver tears brimmed
From the beauty inscrutable old

How may I ease your pain?
Let me be equal with your grief
The resonance of the weep be heard
What grieves your mother's heart

Take it to the somber hills
Obscure it with a throw
And you may not remember but miss it
They will grow in somewhere alone.

MY LOVE, MINE

I was only selfish
To keep you mine
So desperate but not blind
My love, only mine

Possessive if I may be called
To not let the world see your kind
I may be the criminal for your life
As I only wanted you to be mine

So greedy was the world and time
I was afraid and that's my crime
They could steal and keep you
And I had to hide and restrict you

But there I went wrong and right
So suspicious and murderous, I stood-
I strangled you tight;
Not to lose you and your sight

But I knew I was wrong
And I am sorry and you are gone
My selfishness may have ruined you
But it was how I loved

Now look at the brighter side as you always said
And I the darker side as I always claimed
Let you be filled with what you deserve
Your happiness, my resolve

My love, mine
Your love, not mine
Goodbye to that time
Goodbye to your time.

MORAL THIEF

Feelings, these feelings
Gets me and gets us all
From where and when you come
I am dead and I am born

I tried so hard, sometimes to be me
As I was being someone for someone
I hated that, why did I do what I've done
I'm pure but what is this touch
Is it why I always run?

If you know, you can get sick
Why is that you love to leave, the home
You cannot heal from the foreign field
It's too far to remember, who you are
If you're not the son to recall it

Do not depend on the man who you see
He himself cannot see his own back but front
Tomorrow may rise but again fall
Take a step and let the darkness consume all.

APPARITION

"In the field where my thoughts plough,
           your seeds have been graved
forever colluding with my lonely dreams."

THE WINDFLOWER

"She goes up and off in impalpable smoke, while he drank the 60's stroke. Now he must go for the place he does not know. As the man can replicate his own mistake, the endeavor must forget the implacable sweetness of her taste that no longer serves as his own. The aromas or the rumors that leak from the holes of the steady autumn window that sometimes shivers from the teasing's of the dusky wind and if you stare at its emptiness for long and mad to make you think, her roots have already sailed off to another shore and settled for the piers no longer waiting for your isle to call her home. And he will do the same for his roots, will seek another land before, before he is killed by the only man (himself) who feeds on her love each hour; now he must resist his wrinkled bones and forget, for he is unloved and been forgotten by ..Who now belongs to many but not to her own."

PRIDE SWALLOWED ME

The fire that burned from your lips
Has left me in eternal flame
It came from a day and followed me everywhere
And watched me strain all the way

The brightness within your eyes
Has left me discolored and paralyzed
And when those tears fell
I felt my world vanish in disarray

I wanted to hold you and your burden
That made you weak and dismayed
But I didn't and let you drink the ocean of sorrow
And let it burn me to ashes-
I was defeated

I didn't know waters could pierce me
Cleave me into despicable crowded cliché
But in secret I swallowed a prideful man
Who tore me and my fate in sheer misery.

IN MY DISASTER

It's the empty path in the distance that makes an absent heart yearn for someone now and then
It's the certain lonely realization in a secluded place; I hesitate once more to beckon her name,

I was longing for restricted residence; such confined endearment was affecting the very air
Either one of them would bring me straight to one of those days; her smile beneath my face; a rue again

Close my eyes, I feel the breeze- if it was the breath, touched from the lips; I once kissed
Smell the lovely daffodils- plucked it for myself; if I could once alas, grief her scent from her skin where laid in my bed

Wrote her address without direction, in stones from my
footsteps and threw it in the sky holes, thinking I'll never see it
down just the same,
Lost it; farewell was reminded- gravity found myself in terrible
mess-

Waved the signs of ache- in the field collecting rain and I ran
with bare feet and bare hands
It's the cut-bruised misty sunset that leaves me astray to the
place so crowded
How am I to be forgotten from her reminding days; if love
meant before strangers and befell.

TO THE GOING LOVE

Which warmth have I lost now
Never seems to figure out, enough to sleep
What touch have I misled?
My heart forfeited every mistress keep
Oh god! What do you please?
My everything's stolen; for a drifting ship
Shall it to be the loss; my innocent, the nineteen!

A stack of wise age shall be safe in it-
Thus, time to time I get stared by,
Such a sweet melancholy morsel in her eyes
I miss them seeing now both grow
It's the days that I can lack, years from now, oh!

Was I; was it the rest and she the only
Did I gave my all and only love
If it's not, take your step to the strange bed, then
And all that is left is me; somewhere cold, perforated

You're paralyzed, you're alone-
Can only be heard from a frozen mind
Look at your feet, back and forth
Running now into the sea, drowning bold

Goodbye is all they speak
My life, my days and she or me
Let it be, let her be…
Go to sleep…

THE GIRL IN RED

"Sit with me?" she said, before I could glance;
Chairs, table, spoon and everything that I ignored
Not before then I knew, butterflies burnt inside
Like a fuel, not hormones but potions they made
But she spoke further and I didn't understand-
What I understood was her lips with luscious grey;
Touching and teased, moved and placed
Her skin were made with silky thread; blazing-
Draped and enrobed with crimson red
How I imagined, how I'd swim through her depths-
"Would it be the place, my salacious sanctum", I smirked!
She smiled! And the poet grew in desperation and in rush
As he was born from her thighs to her wrist, not the romance,
But every weight could ground hold; opposed and attempted
to escape-

I said, "How many poets failed to verse you and rhyme?"
For not, I sighed within, "to poetry such art be possible?"
-As I quarreled inside.
"I must surrender and beg for her love", her fumes tempted
me! "Love, I suppose I could gift, or the only thing that can be
done to such as art, only thee-"
If not, "How shall I keep her and never be apart?" I strived
alone.
For she said, "Love if, if it's loved, not love if it needs to be
loved-
And I whispered, "You're more than any love, perhaps more
than any magic ever befell."

Amour Fou

"But my roots have already sheltered inside your heart yet you do not speak the verse of love. You knew, for my limbs can stretch further and further away from you like the branches of an oak tree but I still keep wandering in your sea, where your walls have taken stealth shift. Have I not become your lover oh, goddess of beauty? But like me who has spoken the romantic prose and promising vows of lust, has already procured their partners dream; and why must I roam the earth and around your abandoned cities but not your home that keeps your soul somewhere asleep? I want to meet her; will she never take me?"

WORLD AND HER

Pretend you're just a child
Pretend you're lost
But the world doesn't need you
Like I do, in my naked arms
Don't follow them, don't be one
They don't know where you came from
They will steal you, your delicate touch

Oh, world stop holding her, you had your fun
You don't need her, you have all
I am not your follower; do not own her in retribution
You can have my pride but not this love
She is innocent; don't fascinate her hunger

You have seen what weakens us all
But this greed shouldn't justify everyone
Let me have my cure; I have no avarice for this girl
She is pure, and purity is worth dying for.

MEMOIRALISA

"Long is gone and dew is past; remembering you
was the sweetest, as the breathe that touched
your lips, alas!"

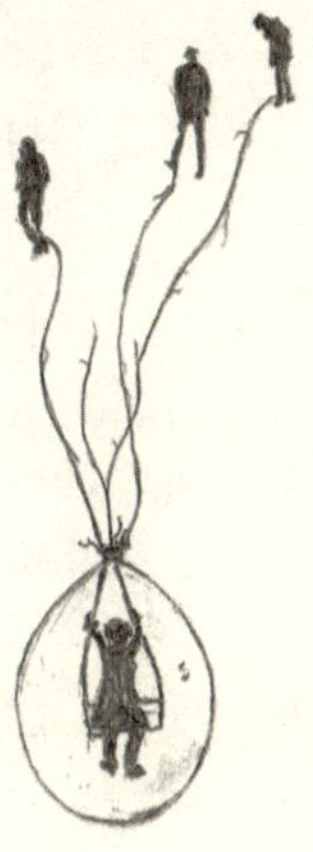

MISANTHROPY

"What if the man you desire cannot remain with you, the man you couldn't chase but only be forgotten because here, he may be seeking his only 'escape', and there were no such thing from the beginning."

HEAVY STEPS

Come again, come again as repeated
Like the kind of warmth that melted the snows with elegance
So desperate the blustery wind, will remind me of my days
Where I've waited for you here again

Winter has gone and the snows too
But I found myself chasing the frosty air
Like a fool, like an imbecile
In the age or for the weary years

The flowers that I love, do not live
And the trees that I shared, shattered long ago
Why is that, why should I be the one to state
Such a dreary and desolate care

I should be on my way and not counting suns-
Up and high the mountain's paths are shaved
In the rivers and in the forest, I should be lost-
For not looking back, I should go ahead.

DYING FLAME IN THE RIVER

Come save me there is a stranger inside of me
It's ripping every part asunder in maudlin
It's twisting my thoughts, breeding in self-delirium
I barely caught my dissembled state; please do not betide she-
Or in blustery act, I will be the victim of every hysterical
crime-seen

Oh experts, so called are here for best at using their legal tool
Now will be published my name at noon
As my lovers they fancy it to read them soon
Now irony must it be, as they call evil to my camouflaged
goodness too
Or I should convince myself; goodness were victims as they
were exiled through.

SMOTHERING WARM HANDS

Who am I, who am I?
Love full of lies!
Like the foreign hands
Who keeps you awake-
Tell me, can you love your strange man
Will you keep his heart alive?
To yours and to mine

Do you know me, do you know him?
If I didn't know you, if I didn't care-
Like the modern city
That leaves you tonight
Tell me, can you perceive this man
Will you tell him, who is he?
Or who is not but of your mind
To me and to time

The dawn seems breaking
And the years still missing
Yet, I'm plucking secrets-
From the twilight of sombre lights
But the stranger keeps his afternoon-
For yours and for mine

Oh, you're such a sly person
You fool me and the nighttime
Please be fair like the literature
Not like the hidden songs;
You dance with crime
But you hide intruders so well
And I keep asking who am I.

TASTE, TOUCH AND SMELL

I sold my angels for the sadness
Now the sadness won't accept trade in return for you
And the winter is coming close, winter of truth
Not the cold I fear but the night sheltering you

Oh blindness, deaf or dumb is it you?
Taking me away from my physical youth
Am I the victim now of my own drug loathe
Making me go numb, choosing to lose
Is this new, is it true?

INTO PARADISE

"Silk thread rushed on my skin, warm fist beneath my chin- it was your world and only mine and where I pretend to sleep, just to keep you with me and none to steal you away from my slip. I knew they were coming; the marching parade on those hills, so these eyes stood guard and the flowers on the wall kept moving.

The jealous rain kept coming and didn't seem to stop. Some were dripping outside and some were leaking from my side while she sang the lullaby of the ever-loving lovers that ran beside the graceful breeze which arrived briskly; the pale green grass skindered- both vanished between the abyss of a horizon that never surfaced again and finally ended with only a word- hush!"

WITH DEATH

"I have no intention of dying old and worn out, my beloved.
The idea is to die young, with all might...even death should
be met with passion, and with little effort...surely, there's this
life & end."

NOT LOVE

"But more than the thoughts of having her, I wanted
to know her and understand how it feels
to swallow up the chaotic world."

SILLY UNDERSTANDING

Life has a way to heal you
And living has it's ruse to wound you
It's with or without you

The sun may differ from yesterday
And the rain may carry on from today
It's with or without you

So sold out, won't you wonder
From everything to the discrete
She said, "Is it all for the change?"

And we pondered to various plain
To make it different nonsense
He said, "If only one can always be the same"

The contents or the subject, we hold it inside
The contemporary secrets and the inner process-
How shall one define or defy?

With the answers within your fabricated question
Each one can savor the satisfaction and take pride
But the stupidity and the acceptance will never side

How long does it take to be born again?
Wise men are dying and the rest are the smile
So long, it's with or without you again.

You and Me

Oh love forget about who we are and who we were
We are travelers now; let's travel far and far away
Rest your skeptical bones and cautious soul today
We will take everything this world has hidden and ever made

Use your every ruse in your search for the need, inside
Tell me your deepest secret where I'll find myself locked up in
your corner's depth
Now did you hear the sound, in our mesh; heavens laid
Sky is barely holding while nature rages on in tempestuous
bliss
Oh, love we are the rolling stone, hold me tight,
Let us roll down again and again

You and me love, let's be insane through sanity
Forget about day and night, madness will befall
Give me your best; give me your secret taste
Let's not return, let's get lost; let's follow the dusk away.

MUSE

"No, I didn't love her for she was broken and needed; I loved
her because of her breaking-

I fell in love with her sadness."

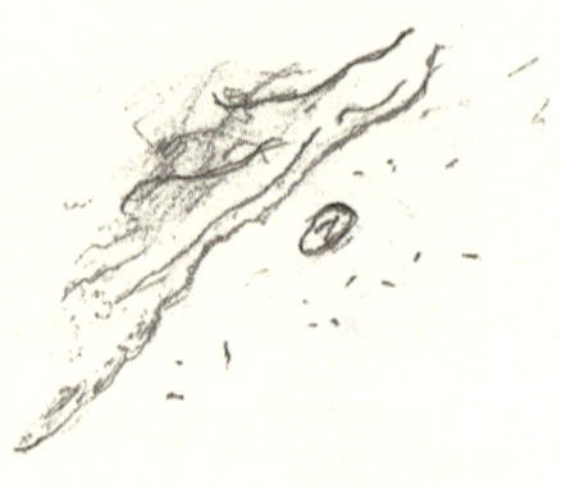

THE SLUMBER

"I would rather enjoy the illusions of sleep instead of waking
up to face the dreadful reality, where I lost you."

DEAD REALITY

So unfair to know after what is done, when it is to be gone
Being without a clue, not even a hunch for a tragedy yet to be
born
So precious, she was mine; didn't know it was the last time

Let the moment slip by, passed through my eye-
Her departure, her physical atmosphere and the untouched
goodbye
So many words left unsaid but then who knew tomorrow was
a different day

How can I explain the madness and seething ache for this fate?
I could have told her everything she meant to me
I would have felt her in my arms, captivating her warmth for
ever to live
She was the one and only flower in my garden, besides my
sleep.

TO BE HERS

"I want to be one of her books. I want to be read like a life not like a page, even if it's dark and mysterious- just like her interest.

> Apparently, it's a seduction to be engraved by her eyes, excavated and submerged through with every line on a paragraph, deeper and deeper as if she is in dire need of uncovering every piece of its sentence, as if there is more to be seen than what it appears- the concentration, her attention. Simply appealing!

Wouldn't it be pleasurable to be held by such touch, delicate movements as if it matters and something so important that it has its own contribution. Yes! Oh the embracement near her breast with her frail fingertips; who keeps unfolding every chapter without any disturbance and distraction. I loved it! I loved the way she read those books. I fancy being one of them someday."

PASSING DEAD SEA

Of all the places I have ever valued more than thriving
It was in the odd and bizarre scene; yours
Where I went every day to taste my emptiness-
Over stitched and mended pieces
I liked it, I loved it a lot
Because I lost and learned the humans, temporary fall!

THE MADNESS

"There there, a conflict splutters inside your flimsy clumsy heart and it feels like the inflating heat of the sun in the desert but its damp, she says..."fuck! I've got wet lungs. It's bilious ", and the infuriating thoughts chewed down like a morsel that lingers around your tongue and sprawls along ... it says...
"run. . .run, it's suicide to stay here"
-"No, it's not. You need to be here"
-"Maybe you do?"
-"No, you don't"
- "Yes...run!"
Let you suffer, they demand; yeah, she holds the company of numerous unembodied experts who debate for her. She says, "Don't play like the boys of temporary cults- I must keep his boarders... but I must run."

FORGET WHERE WE BELONG

Now the storm has took us all, you and me
With the verse, hello... goodbye and so
Have you ever forgotten those?
Those who've forever named our soul-
To path this lonely road,
To return us; to our home...

LOVERS

"Let's meet again like strangers
Don't mind the past,

We can pretend...
All we need are those beginnings, when love meant
everything."

CHAPTER

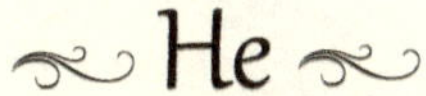 He

"The taste of your soul has marked my flavour and in search
of such, I will travel for eternity again."

THE BOY

"I want to leave you all" he said with the rebellious mind and perhaps, a broken heart? For he was seen walking travesty into the woods, passing the winter flowers that bloom beside the vigorous rivers on the side; last time. He didn't tell me where he should go and when we will meet again. And I didn't bother questioning him, for I knew he had things to forget or maybe people, as he always built hatred for them. But I didn't quite understand for he did not care about the world and his surroundings; what may have tormented his mind and soul at the same time for a person like him, that he pleaded every time to get lost when the sun mocked him with its rays and fluttered his eyes with warmth. He constantly yearned for disappearance."

THE DARK

Father, take my hand
Let us go back to the place where I went alone
Let us erase these memories of your absence
Fill it with your embrace and tell me, you are there
Teach me all the lessons and talk about this cold world
Take away all my empty fascination and empty wishes
Give me hope and dreams and let me grow bold
Cause for this path, now I need a salubrious childhood
But here I stand alone, where no love resides
Heartless it feels, maybe the devil- she calls me too
I want to be saved but there is no room, dreary looming looms!

SECRET SIN

Oh, mother why are you so alone?
Have I not known your grief?
You keep them hidden from our home
Perhaps, words are too sinful to leak;
They won't trade you any remorse
They won't convey your anguish

But what if we tell you, we knew
Too harsh we felt it to convince you-
The love you lost and the home that burns

I wondered once in awhile
Were we too young to let it through?
And the poison you drank all day-
To let it end you

I regret and I am sorry
These hands are too young
And these bones too old-
To save you, my beloved family

NO PILLAR

I lost the family too early
To call, to greed them whole
In search of the memory-
Youth is getting old
In places we live, I still feel alone

Who calls a man weak
When he stood so tall,
Shadows he left behind
His own, he will never show
Now we are just the individual
Who can't retrieve or repair
The childhood with broken toes

I won't deny, I love my very home
Even it is just a house with cracked floors
Some people will never learn what they hold
But I still missed those steps of their sound
Which averted this loneliness- in my young bones
It's just silent as reticent of sister's tears now,
It will fade old, in their soul-
As I continue them, in these limited notes.

ORPHIC

Satirist and pessimist was he known
He was the lover who hated the world
But no love remembered his name
As he found no path, coming back home

Didn't matter, his memories were stolen
Desires some- fated his appearance, dissimulation
And hate was all he could share for you
When you embellished his empty heart
But there were other things to keep him, unheard
A man consumed by wanderlust, he knew how to be gone.

RIVERS AND ROADS

My, my and mine, floating beneath my eyes
Eye, eye and eyes, soaked underneath soaring lies
Tip of the tongue, on top of everyone- she
Drifting and driving, drowning my sun

Why sympathy, your comfort should pity me
And your sentiments are savaged colour-blind
You should see, you should now feel incomplete

No flames I could burn, no rain I could shelter here
In questions of the one; one who doesn't return-
They say nothing to be ever yearned if it is gone
And I would never say, they have never earned

CAN YOU FEEL

Oh boy you're so cruel
How can you be a lover?
You should call yourself sinner!
You made her believe
Her skin like a feather
Her breath so light
In the youth, in your leather
Now what remains is despair
Oh, you must be quite a pretender
She still believes in a lover

Mother, where's your revenge
Don't drink off all the poison
You don't need to prove your strength
I can feel the warmth as it fades
As weak as it always trembles, so fair

The sighs in and out of your tired soul-
Echoes in the corner of your bed
No longer can I see your laugh
Your thin muscles they don't play

The love you believed in
Was not so, never there
Build your hatred mother
You deserve a good end.

FIND ME THE ESCAPE

Fine like those cities, pretty skins on the street
No, not after all the dreams, others seen
I was more than of nature, mountains and trees
I was selfish yet I was content, I cared for nothing
But up on the hills, I remembered
I would escape the time, place or my duties
But the escape I begged; needed more than any fantasy
The truth, I was born within the grasp of the things
And those things could easily wreck my dreams.

SLEEPLESS BOY

Drift away you innocent void vessel
Love is not meant for every growth
Where would you go, you'll never know
Everyone lies and in their own way; don't blame yourself
Just don't feed your emptiness as a whole
Promises are to be made but a curse to follow alone
And if you ever get caught between give and take
Don't kill your heart, it's just how things run here and sold.

BEHIND HIS COATS

Come away, come away
There is a child beneath your man
The sun will come and kiss him
He will shy away and smile
He will forget what he has been
Would you believe it then?
How a love happens to any man

I can tell you ways to keep him
And you need to find the child's home
Where he grew up and you can play?
Without the sun, if in the rain
Come away, come away

COMMENT AIMER

"He requested everyone there to bring him beautiful flowers
that they would find in the savage garden, and the one who
brings the most beautiful one will be victorious. And as his
students rushed and crushed every wildflower blooming there
while seeking the beautiful flowers- certainly many found it,
some were excessively pretty and some were elegantly colorful
and as they all returned with one- one boy came empty handed
and sterned.

He asked: "Did you not find one? Or you didn't find any
flowers beautiful. Why did you come with none?"
And the boy said: "They were all pretty, perhaps prettier than
every other sought in the garden but they were all crushed- the
wildflowers, besides one which was mercifully left unharmed
and I thought, picking up would be the harshest thing I could
do for a mere competition or for my own greed to such
beauty- I let it bloom."

EIGHTY SIX

Too cool to write my own name in her diary

Where strangers feel strange, in strange worry

Too fool to write a song with a word spoken

Where heart, leaves its pieces, in an endless story.

WABI-SABI

There is no lullaby for who doesn't sleep
There is no home for who doesn't stay
There is no song for whose heart doesn't sing
There is no hope for whose eye doesn't dream.

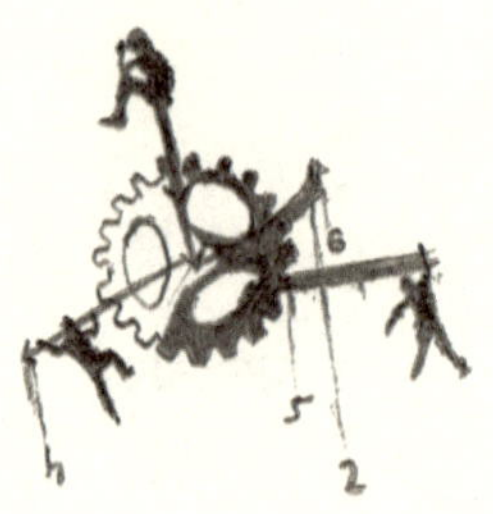

TIME

"How long it had to be to call it forever, or forever
is just the deviation statement of impossible time."

SOMETHING BEHIND

"I think it's the memories that make us come back again and again."

HE FOUND SADNESS

Can you carry me to the mountain side?
I can tell you about the ghost that competes with time
He is old like every man that watches his roof
But he sleeps in the dark like a child in the daylight

"At night, let's meet at the river side, to find", they said
"For who wails the sonnet of his own crime."
Whispers of their heart and some pretty line- spoken
By the touch of their feet and the waters of spring- greeted

They said, "My living spreads among the people and the dead"
"It's misfortune if it's in debts; its life that still complains"
So tell me, can you take me to the side- where lands are not
seen?
I carry their vows and their grief that are now brimmed.

PAINTING SADNESS

Scarlet lips that touched your grips
Shall no more mourn for you-
Will not kiss you anymore,
What if you miss!

Nebulous breath, crimson whiff
Come captivate me, please
It's not wrong to hold such relish
That tore your vital ideal

The dark meanderer stole my soul
My sense here for existence, do not please
So taste me if that may restrain me
My stranger, be with me

Up above the hills and down the streams
Again and everywhere, you must be drifting
Have I not wandered with you to be who we must be?
If we do not succeed, then those shores must vary

It's these feet that do not move
And my bones that do not leak any dreams
My skin can only yearn but do nothing
I can't follow you; it's not that I didn't try
It is what I'll do, if I may ever wish

MY LOVE IS A PIECE OF MY WRECKAGE

The sadness has spread like a blanket of poisons in the sea
It was killing all underneath my shelter, one by one and I
couldn't stop
They died, but it was me, pouring down hell straight to their
sleep
How can I tell the ones who question me- who murdered
through affinity
But would they believe? Beside my rage and my different sides
of pride
I am sad; I am haunted by their sorrow, their longing for me

Here I am claimed by greed; a selfish bliss
And yet with every guilt of not forgiving and deserting a roof-
Squashed, lurched and stopped; repeated sound of terror but
later forgotten
What can I do about this heart or what is this called from
what I feel?
I want to lie! Oh, lying seems comfortable, I always felt good
inside
But can I keep it; can I even do that, have I ever
succeeded...ever?

Wisdom, my wisdom have I ever gained you
But my knowledge seems stupid against my choices; Love
Isn't it called foolish, to talk with your sorrow to be wise
But I guess I was dumb to learn this ruse to write
That! People I love can still hit a dart into me and my
transparency
And make me bleed through the night of dishonesty and
shivering.

DISAPPEAR

"Why do you escape so much from this place, from your own home to somewhere you don't even know. Don't you find loneliness in those strange lands? They don't even remember you."

- "But it's better without people sometimes and it relents me completely when I am on my own- to be a stranger at the same time. It's good to be lost and not found, and what is there to be remembered by all? I don't even want to be reminded.

DIRTY AND DUSTED

Three nights were never home to me
But the distance does not lie
Like my affections, they rush
But my desire to get lost eases me

Is it all about the escape?
Or I am too stubborn for disappearance
Such desperation for- to run
Have I only loved myself?

A little of remorse sold
For a journey I paid
Places I go, places to forget
Will I remember what I loved?
The taste of my days!

LOST 21

Had a talk with myself today, everyday
Played with some numbers, I was too late
I had a thing to take care of, I was frustrated
But life has just begun, it's what they say
Shall I pretend to be old or just a friend?
I can only be young with this dream
The beautiful green- in speed of train
Where will you go? I don't have any place
I can't get off nor can I stay

Can I be afraid of growing old and go home?
If I kill this man and a child shows,
Will he be caged as a murderer or more so
But unlike everyone, I don't want your opulence-
I just want those six to never fade
Only with memories, I may not carry on-
Let me live with them in my own bed
I have a tendency of seeing them around
Can you figure it now- who's dead?

VULNERABLE MAN

Such an expensive path for a cheap taste
An irony caught in an expansive place
But these are the roads where the heavy knee falls-
Where my remedy becomes the dreary outcomes

How shall I come again to this inextricable mess?
Your words have an inevitable phrase which always impairs,
I could not digest; it should emit in hellish ways
Where I have become a dangerous man, threatening itself.

FOR LOVING: DISAPPOINTMENT

Don't leave this man alone
Terrors of destruction, marches this man's hill
And he is all by himself waiting

Said, he would do fine without any
But his death waits for his yelling
And can you let him be?

Did he not give you what you wanted?
Why your hate weighs your memory with him
He says you're all the same, killing him

He doesn't understand, how selfish you people are
Roses for roses and dead for dead?
And for your hell, he should live on?

How abrupt your heart; rejoices then
You insult the same man, once you adored
Then you compare him with your foes

Then what shall be the worth of loving
If nothing can remain but hate-
If not hate, then the absence?

Then he should blame you for this hurt
For every tragedy that shredded him;
For trusting and for loving.

THE LOST TRAVELER

The sun has frozen and shied away
By the clouds of endless maze
The lake has to overflow someday
And the mountains to leak the secret
Ever I envied the long journey of the rivers
I must be quite enraptured by their wilderness
The rain came as I stood wondering
How long have I been blessed?
I need to go again to search these avenues
Beyond the sharpening dictate

THERE BE NO GOODNIGHT

I am lost in this change
Between me and myself- other two
I am quite familiar now with the ghost town
The place we both knew

Always dried up by attachments
And my longings keep loaning you
Now let my travels end at you,
Let no beauty remind me of you

Someday or five years more
I will dream of catching your cold hand
Run barefoot and it will rain soon,
Forever should keep lying
If it foresights any love through past
I wish I never knew the truth

Like once the old man said
Secrets are to be kept if it is secret
And no one complains if no child grows
Like the running in the field
When green grass turns to snow
I hope you know the place we both let go.

TEMPTATION

Escape is like a lost asset
In the blankets of your delusional fumes
No one will sleep, if no one's dreaming
Perhaps, am I asleep by infatuation deep?

This growth belongs to me
But underneath grows your beauty
Alluring my every desire- foreseen
So come to me, replenish me
Dear, you've been my every sad morning

LONELY CHILD

For dust we are, as dust we go
Reckless children of heaven,
Dances with the beast of hell
Beauty of the shadows beneath the line
For the love, you're alone tonight

It's the hate for hate
But not heart for heart
Devil will sing for your pouring eyes
Cover your chaos sleep in the ground
For the warmth, let there be no one
Kiss the coldness in the touch of your crown
No queen shall forbid you and promise you now

"Sometimes, things do not change but our thought does,
Love does not fade but our heart does."

THE AFFLICTION IN THE JOY

"Once before it happened, I thought my heart will sound like the breaking of the bones and the cracking of the walls after the 'heartbreak' - because now and then every poet and every philosopher I adored, spoke so heavy and with such care about it, that it has to be with such destruction and damage that it would sound devastating and so with terror… but I was vaguely disappointed as it didn't, it never did. The unpleasing and unsatisfying fact left me baffled.

It actually sounded like… nothing and nothing but so plain that it is so unfitting, for it has only silence for such great despair and tragedy to the living."

THE INSATIABILITY OF ONE'S

What if a man is not a man before he sweats from his chin
What if his earnings can only be earned and kept by his
struggles
And not by his dream or by his wish, only by his service
Oh I think he has done his best, now he must rest or perhaps
sleep
He must be awake before the desperate dawn and keep on
digging his teeth
But his efforts and his labour are now counted in everyone's
greed
But it's the needs that keep us all on our feet and you think
these limbs run by themselves like the tongue you leak?

He has done for you; he had done for us all
Don't you think what must be done for his own and not for
others?
Because life is one bowl, the porcelain made with delicate
things- it's pretty outside
But we all know, it must break one day; don't dare like it won't
as it starts from inside,
Fill it with what you can; feed from only your dear land

Oh! Wait; there is a risk of brimming out of hand
A piece is good and it's for you, what have you thought?
Why must you seek more than what you deserve?
Be like a man, but don't be his heart... it's absurd
You know, he is rich for his duty but not for his desire and
what he dreams.

SLUMBER AWAY

The sun is down and it's coming
I don't want to wake up
I can't pretend another living

It could rain but pour outside
It could brim and you can see
There are oceans beneath my feet

Perhaps, the merchant of death is generous
Too kind to put my lovers to sleep
Will I see them in my dreams?

My people are traded by the time
And I'm tired- they meant no love
These graves don't wait for any

I will bury you with the song, do not worry
From the bushes and from the trees
I hear the whisper, they say…go to sleep
Go to sleep, you are far too kind to live.

THE POSSESSION

- "You're not a lover! You swallow people. But tell me if you do know?"

-"The possession must proceed, if you really do love them as the whole world waits for you both to be torn asunder. Believe me!"

-"You're a selfish fool. What kind a lover owns his own love? The love has its own space to thrive and give you its taste. Did you not love her at first for her own ways of being and who is the world, if not you?

-"How can one love without the possession? Then they will steal your love like mine!"

-"Perhaps that's why you must be alone! And you're alone!"

TELL MY PRESENT

What will you count after twenty years
If you're not the man to include the friends
What can be lost and be hated-
Or loved, maybe love can remain?
If you're the man with a home again!

If I talk about today and not tomorrow
Will you now understand me or can you try
I will repeat my words and then I can wait
People can climb towers and I can search you in maze,
Often and perhaps unimpressed

My heart wears different emotions one at a time
In the weather of crowded perception;
Each one never seen but the secrets can be leaked
From a mother's garment of wooden tree-
Black silhouette, now all revealed differently; mistakenly

A bunch of lonely people and who was I?
I have been left with emptiness but clear of the past
Something will always be missing and that was it
To discern was the sagacious path of yours,
If it wasn't the review that went awry from the start

It's up to date, the numbers of delay
I'm against the mirror, can't recognize
This seems familiar, these stories of the morning
This town where these homes pretend to be friends
I am feeling weird and do not know anything
This emptiness is blinding and yet it's safe.
What will you choose and what can be of your days.

THERAPY MINE

Or I exclaim in condemnation
But it could be for the last time
The abyss of eternity could arise
And it's not right

Have a taste of its fatigue in procession
Where running ruse will not be able to hold deceit, and hide
Where shall I lock myself?
Love has failed every time

But soon this haughty guy will devastate and cry
Close your eyes and turn yourself to lie
But it could be for the last time
Where things can't be returned while it dies
So when I try: trying to hoax this version abash
You should laugh for me, every time in every line

FOLLOW THE STRANGER

Where the hollow hero runs
From the land of belief
Your love was the truth
Yet mystery conquered him
You say a free man roams the earth
Tell me who escaped nostalgia's advert,
The man with a dream or without love,
Cultured being or heartless fall
Oh, life can be so meaningful
And here sometimes it reveals nothing at all

~2016~